Arya's Ocean Adventure

Written By: Nati Batool
Illustrations By: Desin E.

Thank you for supporting Arya's Wishes, where 100% of the proceeds will go towards making a real difference in the lives of those in need.
Visit us at: www.aryaswishes.org.

In the deep blue ocean, lived Arya so sweet,
With hair like seaweed, and fast-moving feet.
She loved watermelons, grew them with care,
In her garden so lush, they were beyond compare.

One bright sunny day, Arya set out,
With a basket of melons, she swam all about.
Through coral reefs, she sang a song,
Her voice echoed sweetly, as she swam along.

First came Danny, a dolphin so blue,
He felt he wasn't the fastest, feeling quite rue.
Arya gave him a melon, said with delight,
"Enjoy the journey, Danny, and all will be right."

Next was Tina, a turtle in plight,
Worried for her family, through day and night.
Arya handed a melon, said with a grin,
"Live in the moment, Tina, let joy in."

Then came Oliver, an octopus grumpy,
Feeling quite lonely, his mood was so jumpy.
Arya shared her melon, with a warm glow,
"Friendship takes time, Oliver, just let it grow."

Along swam Arya, to Penny the shy,
A pufferfish scared, too afraid to try.
She gave Penny a melon, said "Face your fear,
Believe in yourself, and courage will appear."

Next met Sammy, a seahorse so small,
He felt insignificant, hardly noticed at all.
Arya offered a melon, with a soft plea,
"You're special, Sammy, just wait and see."

Then came Carl, a crab rushing by,
Always in a hurry, never stopping, oh my!
Arya gave him a melon, said with cheer,
"Life is like a watermelon, savor each bite, my dear."

After a long day, Arya swam back,
Feeling fulfilled, with her basket no longer packed.
She'd helped her friends see the beauty around,
In the simple joys that always abound.

In her garden, Arya sat with delight,
Watching her watermelons growing in the light.
Surrounded by friends, in the ocean so deep,
She lived life to the fullest, with lessons to keep.

About Us

Our little one passed away in 2020 leaving behind her strength and selflessness. She was a force that impacted our lives in many different ways during the global pandemic and still teaches us lessons every day (even if we don't know it). Arya made us understand that life is too short and it is best to keep giving to any being in need. We wish to keep her journey going with this organization.

Our Mission

We aim to give back to the community as we encourage people to care about each other and highlight unity and charity amidst **diversity**. We started raising funds to benefit the local shelters and we plan to continue this advocacy as we dedicate our time and expertise. Arya's Wishes catalyzes personal and social change in all-encompassing groups to champion their lives and meet all their physical, emotional, mental, and financial needs.